D1710850

a. w

Funny Number Tricks

Easy Magic with Arithmetic

By Rose Wyler & Gerald Ames • Pictures by Tālivaldis Stubis

PARENTS' MAGAZINE PRESS • NEW YORK

CONTENTS

Library of Congress Cataloging in Publication Data
Wyler, Rose.
    Funny number tricks.
    SUMMARY: Simple mathematical tricks that will
make you look like a magician.
    1. Mathematical recreations—Juvenile literature. [1.
Mathematical recreations] I. Ames, Gerald, joint au-
thor. II. Stubis, Tālivaldis, 1926-   . III. Title.
QA95.W94   793.7'4   76-3439
ISBN 0-8193-0846-3   ISBN 0-8193-0847-1 lib. bdg.

THE WIZARD OF 1-2-3

Hi! Ali Baba from Abra Cadabra.
Hi! Wizard of Numbers.
(That's you.)
Your hat is funny,
and your tricks will be, too.
How you fool people!
You can guess any number they think of.
You add like mad.
Big numbers, small,
you handle them all.

Take a bow, Ali Baba,
and show what you can do.

Ali Adds—and How!

Here is your magic adding trick.
Set out five slips of paper
with different numbers on each side.
Let your friend turn over a slip
behind your back.
Now a number is changed,
and you don't know what the new one is.
Can you add the numbers anyhow?
You do, and the sum is right!

The Secret:

Write these numbers on the slips—
1 on the first slip
and **2** on the other side,
3 on the second slip
and **4** on the other side,
and so on up to **9** and **10**.
Set out the slips with even numbers up.
These numbers add up to **30**.

When any slip is turned over,
the new number is one less than the old.
So you know the sum is **30 − 1**.
It is always **29**.

Ali Knows His Dominoes

Who can tell how a game of dominoes will end?
You can.

Give your friends the dominoes.
Have them line up the dominoes
the way they are lined up in a game.
What numbers will come out
at the ends of the line?

Write down two numbers.
Let's say you write **5** and **3**.
When all the dominoes are in line,
the numbers at the ends are—
5 and **3**!

The Secret:

Before you start,
take out a domino and hide it.
If you take out the one
with **5** and **3** on it,
then **5** and **3** will come out at the ends.

The trick works with other dominoes, too.
But it does not work with a double.

Four Fourths Equal One

$\frac{4}{4} = 1.$ Prove it, Ali Baba.

Hold up a strip of paper about six inches long.
Tear it across the middle.
Say, "This gives us **2** halves."

Then tear the halves across.
"And this gives us **4** fourths."

Now show that **4** fourths equal one.
Pull out the paper and—the strip is whole again!

The Secret:

Prepare a strip of paper
about twelve inches long.
Fold it in half.
Then fold one of the halves this way.

When you do the trick,
keep the folded half hidden in your hand.
After tearing the other half,
keep the torn pieces hidden.
Then pull out the untorn part of the strip,
and it seems that the pieces
are all put together again.

The Magic Q

Make the **Q** with buttons.
Put **6** buttons in the tail
and **16** in the ring.
Have someone choose a number from **8** to **16**
and count it out on the **Q**.
You don't know the number,
and you don't watch the counting.

Your friend must start at the tip of the tail,
then go around the ring to the left
until the chosen number is reached.
On that button, your friend
begins counting the same number
in the opposite direction around the ring.

Where will the count end?
You point to a button,
and it is the right one!

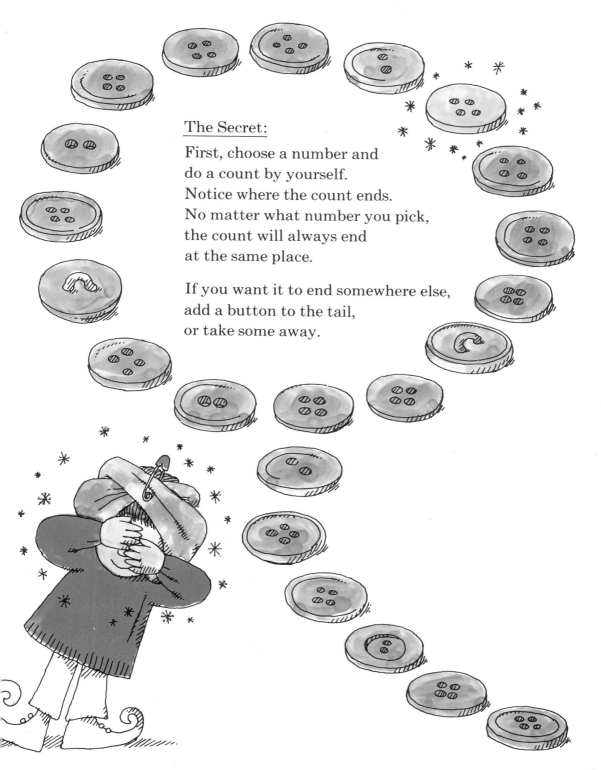

The Secret:

First, choose a number and
do a count by yourself.
Notice where the count ends.
No matter what number you pick,
the count will always end
at the same place.

If you want it to end somewhere else,
add a button to the tail,
or take some away.

The Mystery Count

Give your friend Mary a deck of cards. Say, "Pick a card. Don't let me see it, but I'll figure out the one you picked."

Mary takes a card, looks at it, then lays it face down on top of the deck (also face down).

Then you cut the deck
and put the lower half on top.

Next, turn up the cards, one by one.
Count them out loud as you turn them.
You stop at a certain card and—
it is the right card!

The Secret: *

Before you start, look at the bottom card of the deck.
Say it is the **2** of hearts.
When you cut the deck
and put the lower half on top,
the **2** of hearts will come before Mary's card.

* Watch for it as you count out the cards.
The counting is just to puzzle your friend.

*

*

Clockwork

Point to a clock and say,
"Pick two opposite numbers on the clock.
Add them, tell me the sum,
and I'll guess the numbers you picked."

Billy picks a pair of numbers
and gives you the sum—**16**.
Without looking at the clock, you say,
"Billy, you picked **5** and **11**."
Of course that is right!

The Secret:

A clock has six pairs of opposite numbers.
Going from **1** to **6**, the pairs add up to
8, **10**, **12**, **14**, **16**, and **18**.
Remember these sums.
When your friend names one of them,
you can tell which numbers he picked.

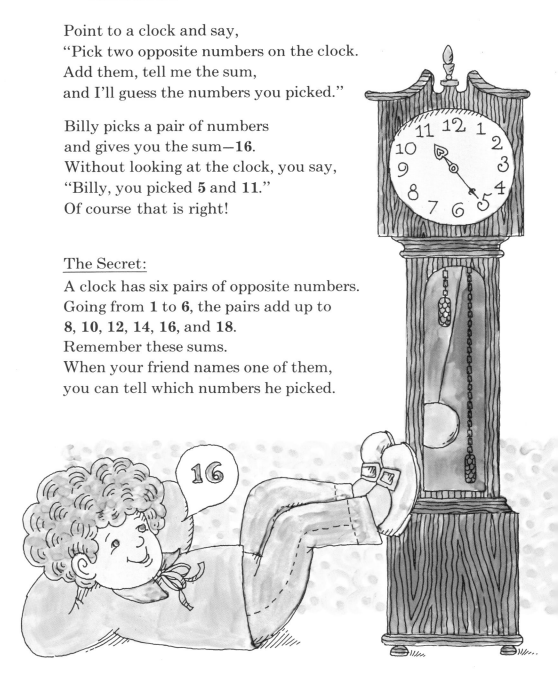

Then try this.
Say, "Take a pair of opposite numbers,
subtract the smaller number from the larger,
and I'll tell you how much is left."

The Secret:
The answer is always **6**.

Spoof knows a lot of jokes and tricks.
Goof always falls for them.
Your friends will, too.
When you do the spoofing,
they will do the goofing.
And you will all have fun together.

SPOOF
AND
GOOF

Spoofy-Goofy Counting

Spoof: How many fingers do you have?
Goof: Ten.
Spoof: Wrong! You have **11**. Count them.
    (Goof counts **10** fingers.)
Spoof: You missed one. Let me count.
    (He takes Goof's right hand
    and counts backward.)
    Ten, nine, eight, seven, six.
    (Then he takes Goof's left hand.)
    And **5** makes **11**.

Counting by 3's

Spoof: Can you count by **3**'s?
Goof: Sure. **3, 6, 9, 12.**
Spoof: Can you count to **11** by **3**'s?
Goof: No, and neither can you.
Spoof: Oh yes I can.
    I start with two—**2, 5, 8, 11.**

What Comes Next?

Spoof: What comes after nine?
Goof: Ten.
Spoof: What comes after ninety-nine?
Goof: A hundred.
Spoof: What comes after nine hundred ninety-nine?
Goof: A thousand.
Spoof: What comes after nine thousand ninety-nine?
Goof: Ten thousand.
Spoof: Wrong. Nine thousand one hundred.

(9,099, then **9,100)**

You fell for it again!

Goof Misses the Bus

Spoof: Here is a counting test. Ready?

Goof: Okay.

Spoof: A bus starts out empty.

At the first stop it picks up **10** people.

At the next stop **5** get off

and **2** get on.

At the next stop **4** get on

and **1** gets off.

At the next stop **2** get on.

At the last stop **5** get off.

How many stops did the bus make?

Goof: I don't know.

I was counting the people.

Spoof: Too bad. That's why

you missed the bus!

Change a Square

(Spoof takes **12** buttons
and makes a square
with **4** buttons on each side.)
Spoof: Here is a square—and a puzzle.
   Can you change the square
   into a shape
   with **5** buttons on each side?
   (Goof thinks about it.)
Goof: I give up.
Spoof: It's easy. Just do this.
   (Spoof makes a triangle.)

25

Write a Number

Spoof: Think of a number.
Don't tell me what it is.
Just write it down,
and I'll write down a bigger one.
This is what Spoof writes:

How Many Pennies?

(Spoof has **10** pennies.
He puts them on the cover of a magazine.)
Spoof: Tell me how many pennies there are,
and you can have them all.
Goof: There are **10** pennies.
Spoof: Are you sure? Count again.
(Spoof pours the pennies into Goof's hands,
and Goof counts them.)
Goof: Why, there are **13**!

The Secret:
Hide **3** pennies under the magazine cover.
They slide out with the **10** on top.

Puzzle of the Six Glasses

(Spoof takes six glasses
and lines them up in a row.
The first three are filled with water.
Glasses **4**, **5**, and **6** are empty.)
Spoof: This is what you must do.
    Move just one glass, and change the line-up
    so every other glass will be an empty one.
    (Goof thinks about it, then gives up.)

Spoof: It's easy.
    (He picks up glass number **2**,
    pours the water into glass number **5**,
    and puts glass number **2**
    back where it was.)

Inchy the Inchworm

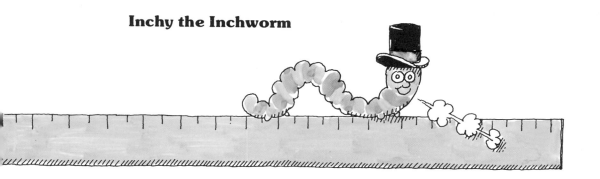

(Spoof pretends to put something on a ruler.)

Spoof: This is my pet, Inchy the inchworm.

Let's see how fast he goes.

If he goes an inch in **1** second,
how far will he go in **10** seconds?

Goof: **10** inches.

Spoof: And if he goes **2** inches a second,
how far will he go in **10** seconds?

Goof: **20** inches.

Spoof: Okay, Inchy, start!

Oh! His hat fell off. Here, hold it.
(Spoof pretends to pick up the hat
and hand it to Goof.)

Spoof: You think I'm crazy, don't you?

Goof: Yes.

Spoof: Well, what about you?

You're the one holding Inchy's hat!

Now for some tricks
you can practice with friends.
Work together,
and when you are good at the tricks,
have a show—a Funny Numbers Fair.
Here is the program—

THE
FUNNY
NUMBERS
FAIR

starring

Madame Puff—She Breathes Numbers

Super Kid and His Super Memory

The Sage Who Tells Your Age

Fingal and His Educated Finger

Sniff, the Arithmetical Dog

Chief Owatta's Ghost

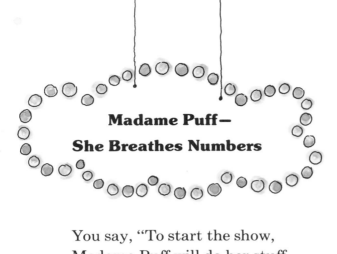

Madame Puff—
She Breathes Numbers

You say, "To start the show,
Madame Puff will do her stuff.
She solves problems
just by blowing on a mirror.
Bob, pick a number for Madame Puff.
Pick one between **10** and **19**.
Write it down, but don't tell what it is."

Bob writes down a number.
"Now add the two digits of your number."
Bob adds.
"Take the sum and subtract it from your number.
What does that leave?
Madame Puff, please give us the answer."

Madame Puff blows on her mirror.
As it fogs up from her breath,
part of the glass stays clear,
forming the number **9**.
"That's right!" says Bob.
He shows what he wrote.

$$17$$
$$1 + 7 = 8$$
$$17 - 8 = 9$$

The Secret:

Whatever number between **10** and **19** is picked,
the answer is **9**.
To make the **9** show on the mirror,
mix some detergent with water,
dip in your finger, and write **9**.

Put the mirror in the refrigerator to cool.
Then, when Madame Puff blows on the mirror,
the glass will fog up, but the **9** will stay clear.

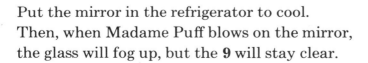

Super Kid and His Super Memory

Tell everybody, "Meet Super Kid.
He can remember a string of twenty numbers."

Write down a string like this—
    32572910112358314594.
Show it to Super Kid,
then take the paper away.

"Now, Super Kid, do you remember all those numbers?
Let's see if you can write down the same ones."
Super Kid writes on another sheet of paper.
Hold up the two papers with the strings of numbers.
The numbers are the same!

<u>The Secret:</u>

The string of numbers is made like this:
Add the first two to get the third.
Add the second and third to get the fourth.
Add the third and fourth to get the fifth,
and so on.

To repeat the string of numbers,
Super Kid just starts with the same first two,
and gets all the rest by adding.

Whenever a sum has two digits—say **10** or **12**—
he drops the **1**, and uses only the **0** or **2**.

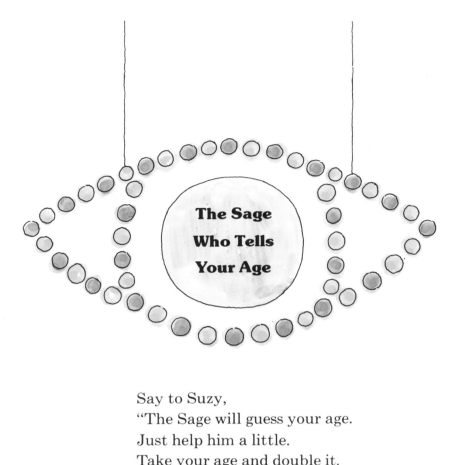

**The Sage
Who Tells
Your Age**

Say to Suzy,
"The Sage will guess your age.
Just help him a little.
Take your age and double it.
Now, take the sum
and multiply it by **10**.
What does that make?"
Suzy says **180**.

Then you ask the Sage:
"Well, Sage, how old is Suzy?"
"She's **9**," says the Sage.
Suzy is surprised.
"How did you figure it out?"
she says.

The Secret:

Here are the figures—

9 + 9 = 18
10 × 18 = 180
180 ÷ 2 = 90
90 with the **0** left off gives **9**

The trick works with any age.
Try it and see.

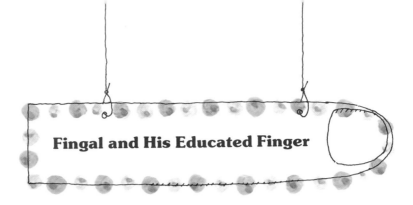

Fingal and His Educated Finger

Say, "Meet Fingal of the educated finger.
He can feel the numbers on a deck of cards."
Have someone shuffle the cards.
Fingal takes them and puts them in a bag.

Have someone else ask for a number from **1** to **10**.
Suppose he asks for **6**.
Fingal feels the cards in the bag,
then he pulls out two cards—a **2** and a **4**.

$$2 + 4 = 6.$$

<u>The Secret</u>:

Before the show,
Fingal takes four cards out of the deck—
an ace, which stands for **1**, and a **2**, **4**, and **8**—
and hides them in the bag.
Nobody knows they are there.

When Fingal puts the deck in the bag,
he slips the four cards on top.
He keeps them in order—**1**, **2**, **4**, **8**.

If someone asks for **1**, **2**, **4**, or **8**,
he just pulls out the right card.
For **3**, **5**, **6**, **7**, **9**, or **10**,
he pulls out the two or three cards
needed to make up
the sum.

Sniff, the Arithmetical Dog

For this trick, you need a helper—and a dog.
Say, "This is Sniff, the arithmetical dog.
He counts toothpicks just by smelling them."

Ask someone to take any number
of toothpicks from **1** to **12**.
Then you and Sniff turn your backs.
"Don't look, Sniff."
Your helper covers the toothpicks with a cup.
You and Sniff turn around.

Have Sniff sniff at the cup.
"Okay, Sniff, how many toothpicks
are under the cup? Speak!"
If Sniff won't bark,
bark for him—"*Arf, arf, arf.*
Sniff says **3**."

You lift the cup and—
there are **3** toothpicks under it!

The Secret:

Your helper places the cup a certain way.
The handle points like the hour hand on a clock.
It points to where the **3** would be.
For **9**, it would point the opposite way.

Chief Owatta's Ghost

Three Indians sit around a drum (a big cooking pot).
One says, "This was the drum of the great chief, Owatta.
He played it when he was alive.
Now his ghost plays the drum."

The Indians call:
"Hail, Chief Owatta of the Numbers Tribe."
Boom-boom goes the drum,
yet no one is touching it.

An Indian says, "Chief Owatta speaks.
Owatta, how many Indians are here?"
Boom-boom-boom goes the drum—**3**.

"If each of us catches **2** wild turkeys,
how many turkeys will we have?"
Boom-boom, boom-boom, boom-boom—**6**.
"How many turkey legs will there be to share?"
The drum beats **12**.
"How many legs will each of us get?"
The drum beats 4:

"If we dig a hole for the bones,
and it is **3** feet wide and **2** feet deep,
how much dirt is in the hole?"
This time the drum is silent.
"Owatta, how much dirt is in the hole?"
"None," calls a voice.
"That is why my drum says nothing."

A fourth Indian steps out from behind a door.
He holds a drum like the one on the floor.
The three Indians bow and greet him.
"Hail, Chief Owatta! Owatta ghost!"

Then they all dance and chant:
"We add what we have,
We divide it and share.
We know our numbers
So we always are fair.
Hooray for our tribe!
Math is our friend.
We've had a good show,
But now it must
     END."